SOUTHERN'S
**SOUTH WESTERN
MEMORIES**

SOUTHERN'S SOUTH WESTERN MEMORIES

Robert Antell

LONDON

IAN ALLAN LTD

First published 1977

ISBN 0 7110 0824 8

© Ian Allan Ltd 1977

Designed by R. Antell

Published by Ian Allan Ltd, Shepperton, Surrey, and printed
in the United Kingdom by
Ian Allan Printing Ltd.

Below: One of the last regular M7 0-4-4Ts No 30667
works on the Seaton branch between Colyton and
Colyford in September 1967./*M J Esau*

Contents

Introduction

The Southern Region had until 1964 a well-tailored rail network to meet local needs west of Exeter and south-east Devon, and a fast main line linked North Cornwall and Devon to the rest of the Southern system and Waterloo, 174 miles away from the County Town. Fast West of England express trains, including the famous 'Atlantic Coast Express', gave a spectacular show of power west of Salisbury as they sped down one steep incline and struggled up the next. Honiton and Hewish Banks sorted out the men from the boys on many a footpate and made the line one of the most gruelling and fascinating main lines in the country.

The photographs in this pictorial album have been laid out is six sections, starting at the London end of the West of England main line and then covering all Southern lines west of Salisbury, concluding with 'the odd one out', the Lynton & Barnstaple Railway, the small narrow gauge line inherited by the Southern Railway in 1923, which ran for 19 miles across the foothills of Exmoor to the twin towns of Lynton and Lynmouth. Unfortunately this line was closed in 1935, 13 years before the Southern Region was formed.

After the reorganisation in 1964, all Southern lines west of Wilton were handed over to the Western Region and within two years all Southern Region trains through to the west of Exeter had been suspended, although trains continue to run between Exeter and Waterloo. They are now required to call at all stations that remain open west of Salisbury, and this section of a once proud main line has been converted largely to single track. The Exmouth branch still remains via Exmouth Junction, Barnstaple is the passenger terminal for the whole of North Devon, and Gunnislake is reached via Plymouth. Three freight only lines also remain; Barnstaple-Meeth, Coleford Junction-Meldon Quarry and the Wenford Bridge line now reached via Bodmin Road.

Below: Rebuilt 'Mechant Navy' Class No 35029 *Ellerman Line* races through Clapham Cutting with a down West of England Express in May 1964./*J Scrace*

Above: Rebuilt 'Merchant Navy' Class No 35026 *Lamport and Holt line* in August 1964 at the head of the down 'Atlantic Coast Express' between Templecombe and Milborne Port./*Paul Riley*

Left: LNER Peppercorn A2 No 60532 *Blue Peter* heads a Waterloo-Exeter LCGB Commemorative Railtour up Hewish Bank in August 1966./*M Pope*

The West of England Service

SOUTHERN

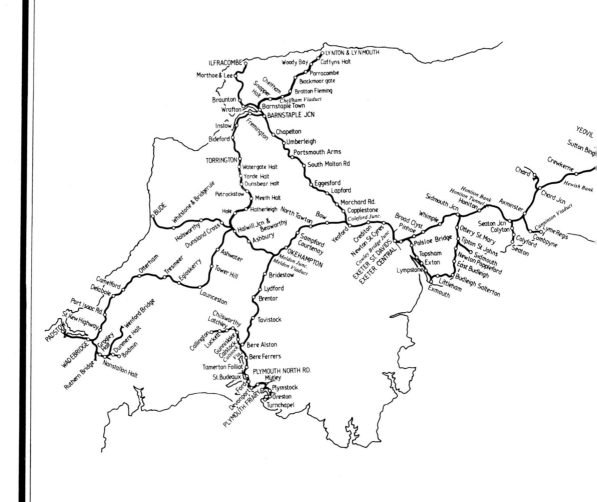

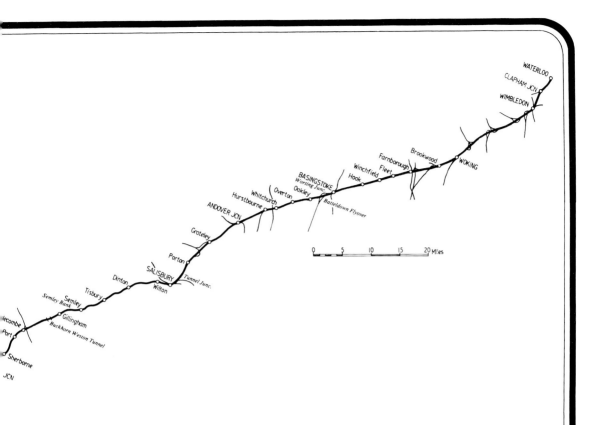

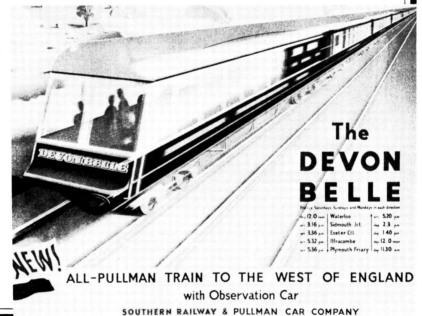

Right: A poster used to advertise the new all-Pullman *'Devon Belle'* with a special observation car introduced by the Southern Railway in 1947./*British Railways*

The
DEVON
BELLE

arr 12.0 noon	Waterloo	dep	5.20 pm
arr 3.16 pm	Sidmouth Jct	dep	2.3 pm
arr 3.36 pm	Exeter Ctl	dep	1.40 pm
arr 5.32 pm	Ilfracombe	dep	12.0 noon
arr 5.36 pm	Plymouth Friary	arr	11.30 am

NEW!

ALL-PULLMAN TRAIN TO THE WEST OF ENGLAND
with Observation Car
SOUTHERN RAILWAY & PULLMAN CAR COMPANY

The West of England Main Line

Below: 'Warship' Class 42 No D803 *Albion* prepares to
leave with the 13.00 Waterloo-Exeter train in February
1971./*J H Cooper-Smith*

Above: 'West Country' Class No 34094 *Mortehoe* approaches Vauxhall with the 11.15 West of England express in June 1959./*P H Groom*

Right: 'Warship' Class 42 No D817 *Foxhound* heads the down 12.00 Exmouth and Sidmouth train through Clapham cutting in August 1965./*J Scrace*

Bottom right: 'Merchant Navy', Class No 35021 *New Zealand Line* speeds the 'Devon Belle' through Wimbledon bound for the West Country in the early fifties./*R Russell*

Above: 'Merchant Navy' Class No 35008 *Orient Line* in experimental blue livery leaves Woking with an Exeter express in February 1950. /*Pursey C Short*

Left: Hymek Class 35 No D7038 arrives at Woking with the 13.08 train for Exeter in May 1970./*J Scrace*

Above right: Rebuilt 'Merchant Navy' Class No 35006 *Peninsular & Oriental Line* races past Pirbright for Exeter in July 1964./*J H Patience*

Right: Rebuilt 'Merchant Navy' Class No 35009 *Shaw Savill* takes the Torrington section of the 'Atlantic Coast Express' through Farnborough in August 1963./*A W Martin*

Left: 'West Country' Class No 34015 *Exmouth* passes Fleet with an excursion train for Waterloo in September 1966./*A D McIntyre*

Below left: Rebuilt 'Battle of Britain' Class No 34059 *Sir Archibald Sinclair* passes Winchfield with the 10.45 Waterloo-Seaton train in August 1961./*J C Beckett*

Right: 'West Country' Class No 34013 *Okehampton* waits at Basingstoke with a local train for Salisbury in September 1967./*K P Lawrence*

Below: 'Lord Nelson' Class No 30864 *Sir Martin Frobisher* takes a Waterloo-Salisbury train under the up Southampton line at Battledown flyover. The physical junction of these two lines is at Worting one mile eastwards. /*Derek Cross*

Above left: 'West Country' Class No 34103 *Calstock* pulls away from Andover Junction with a stopping train to Salisbury in August 1964./*P Strong*

Left: LNER Class A4 No 4498 *Sir Nigel Gresley* heads an A4 preservation society tour approaching Porton in June 1967./*J Scrace*

Above: Un-rebuilt 'West Country' Class No 34023 *Blackmore Vale* leaves Salisbury with the WRS 'Farewell to Steam' tour in June 1967./*D E Canning*

Left: 'West Country' Class No 34002 *Salisbury* heads a railtour through Tunnel Junction, Salisbury in June 1966./*V L Murphy*

Above: Rebuilt 'Battle of Britain' Class No 34082 *615 Squadron* hauls an up West of England express past Tunnel Junction in August 1964./*Paul Riley*

Above: 'West Country' Class No 34036 *Westward Ho* leaves Salisbury with a West of England express in April 1964./*P Strong*

Left: An unidentified 'Merchant Navy' receives attention and changes crew at Salisbury on the westbound 'Atlantic Coast Express'./*Ian Allan Library*

Right: The engine crew attend to their charge's needs at Salisbury. /*J N Westwood*

Rebuilt 'West Country' Class No 34001 *Exeter* takes over from 34015 *Exmouth* for the final stage of a privately sponsored train to Waterloo at Salisbury in January 1966./*R L Sewell*

Above left: 'Western' Class 52 No 1039 *Western King* speeds through heavy rain on the outskirts of Salisbury with the down 'Cornish Riviera Express'. The train was diverted from Paddington via Reading and Basingstoke due to a derailment at Stoke Canon in July 1969./*Ian Allan Library*

Left: Rebuilt 'Merchant Navy' Class No 35025 *Brocklebank Line* approaches Wilton with the 17.50 Exeter to Waterloo train in June 1963./*I A Johns*

Above: 'Merchant Navy' Class No 35009 *Shaw Savill* speeds an up Plymouth-Waterloo express between Dinton and Wilton in September 1964./*G F Heiron*

Above: Class U1 2-6-0 No 31908 arrives at Dinton with a Salisbury-Exeter stopping train in August 1952. /A C U Kendall

Left: Class S15 4-6-0 No 30845 climbs the 1 in 100 incline to Semley with a heavy goods train bound for Salisbury in February 1962. /G A Richardson

Above right: Class S15 No 30832 approaches Buckhorn Weston with a down freight train. /Ivo Peters

Right: LNER Class A4 No 60024 *Kingfisher* emerges from Buckhorn Weston tunnel with an up 'A4 Preservation Society' special in March 1966. /Tim Stephens

The approach to Buckhorn Weston tunnel, (*left*) Rebuilt 'Merchant Navy' Class No 35023 *Holland Afrika Line* heads the 'Devon Rambler' excursion in June 1966. (*Below*) Just two years later two Class 33s Nos 6575 and 6563 head the 8.50 Brighton–Exeter through train over the new single track layout./*Ivo Peters*

Rebuilt 'Merchant Navy' Class No 35024 *East Asiatic Company* awaits the right-away from Templecombe as an up train enters the station behind 'West Country' Class No 34106 *Lydford./Paul Riley*

Left: Stanier Class 5 No 45493 and 'West Country' Class No 34100 *Appledore* head west from Templecombe with an LCGB Excursion in July 1966./*Ivo Peters*

Below left: 'West Country' Class No 34021 *Weymouth* reaches the top of a 1 in 100 incline on the approach to Milborne Port with a down Ilfracombe express in August 1964./*Paul Riley*

Top right: Rebuilt 'Merchant Navy' Class No 35020 *Bibby Line* races through Yeovil Junction with the up 'Atlantic Coast Express' in October 1961./*Harold Ball*

Centre right: Rebuilt 'West Country' Class No 34100 *Appledore* and Class 5 No 45493 leave Yeovil Junction for Pen Mill with the LCGB 'Green Arrow' railtour in July 1966. /*M J Messenger*

Bottom right: Yeovil shed and Town station in the summer of 1964./*M J Fox*

Left: Class S15 No 30829 pulls into Axminster with a stopping train for Exeter./*J Davenport*

Centre left: Class 2MT No 41206 pilots No 41291 between Axminster and Seaton Junction with the LCGB East Devon railtour in March 1965. /*Tim Stephens*

Bottom left: 'Battle of Britain' Class No 34074 *46 Squadron* restarts the 9.35 Exeter-Waterloo semi-fast away from Seaton Junction in July 1962./*D Ian Wood*

Right: Rebuilt 'West Country' Class No 34093 *Saunton* makes heavy work of its climb up the 1 in 80 Honiton Bank with the 11.45 Yeovil-Exeter stopping train in July 1962./*D Ian Wood*

Bottom right: 'West Country' Class No 34109 *Sir Trafford Leigh-Mallory* gracefully climbs Honiton Bank with a Brighton-Plymouth train in the early 60s./*D Cross*

Left: 'Battle of Britain' Class No 34086 *219 Squadron* emerges from Honiton tunnel with an SO Ilfracombe-Waterloo train in August 1964.
Ivo Peters

Right: Rebuilt 'Merchant Navy' Class No 35022 *Holland-America Line* climbs to Honiton tunnel with the down 'Atlantic Coast Express' in September 1964./*Paul Riley*

Centre right: 'West Country' Class No 34030 *Watersmeet* heads the down 11.30 Brighton-Plymouth train through Sidmouth Junction past a Class S15 4-6-0 No 30842 with an up freight train in September 1958./*K L Cook*

Bottom right: 'Merchant Navy' Class No 35020 *Bibby Line* pulls away from Sidmouth Junction towards Exeter in August 1952./*Ian Allan Library*

Above: 'Battle of Britain' Class No 34065 *Hurricane* heads east towards Sidmouth Junction with a train from Exeter Central to Yeovil./*John Parsons*

Left: 'Battle of Britain' Class No 34072 *257 Squadron* pulls away from Pinhoe with an Exeter Central Honiton train in June 1963./*M J Fox*

Above right: Rebuilt 'Merchant Navy' Class No 35026 *Lamport and Holt Line* climbs out of Exeter Central with a return special to Waterloo in September 1966. /*R L Sewell*

Right: 'Merchant Navy' Class No 35025 *Brocklebank Line* heads the up 'Atlantic Coast Express' past Exmouth Junction box in August 1952./*A G Dixon*

'West Country' Class
No 34038 *Lynton* waits at
Exeter Central with an up
train in August 1955.
/John Robertson

41

Above: 'Lord Nelson' Class No 30861 *Lord Anson* pulls out of Exeter Central with an SCTS 'South-Western Limited' special in September 1962./*R G Turner*

Left: 'Warship' Class No D825 *Intrepid* restarts the Waterloo–bound 'Atlantic Coast Express' out of Exeter Central on Friday 4 September 1964. /*R W Hawkins*

Above right: To mark the Centenary celebrations at Exeter on Tuesday 19 July 1960, a 'Beattie Well Tank' stands at Exeter Central. These engines were first introduced in 1874 and finished their long run in service on the Wenford Bridge Line in Cornwall./*Ivo Peters*

Right: Class Z 0-8-0T No 30955 assists Class N No 31844 from Exeter St Davids into the Central station with a heavy goods train./*J B Bucknall*

Left: 'West Country' Class No 34015 *Exmouth* leaves
Exeter Central for the loco shed at Exmouth Junction on
the first of a series of special 'Last trains to Exeter'
in January 1966./*John A M Vaughan*

Above: 'Battle of Britain' Class No 34060 *25 Squadron*
climbs to Exeter Central with the 8.15 Plymouth Friary-
Exeter Central train in September 1958.
/*Colin P Walker*

The South East Devon Branch Lines

Below: A dmu forms the 15.40 train to Lyme Regis at
Axminster in August 1964./*Ian G Holt*

Above: Ex-LSWR 0415 Class 4-4-2T No 30583 climbs out of Axminster with the 12.33 train to Lyme Regis in September 1957./*J C Beckett*

Right: Headed by Class 2MT No 41206 the LCGB 'East Devon Railtour' crosses Cannington Viaduct between Combpyne and Lyme Regis on its return to Axminster and is assisted at the rear by No 41291 in February 1965. /*D H Ballantyne*

Bottom right: Class 0415 No 30584 arrives at Lyme Regis with a train from Axminster in April 1960. /*J C Beckett*

Left: Class 1400 0-4-2T
No 1442 waits at Seaton
Junction with a train to
Seaton in February
1964./*W C Sumner*

Below left: No 1442 seen
approaching Seaton
Junction with an auto train
in March 1965.
/*Gerald T Robinson*

Right: Class 1400
No 1450 pulls away from
Colyton with the 14.06
train to Seaton Junction in
March 1965.
/*W L Underhay*

Below: No 1412 seen
leaving Colyford for
Seaton on a late afternoon
train in February
1965./*W G Sumner*

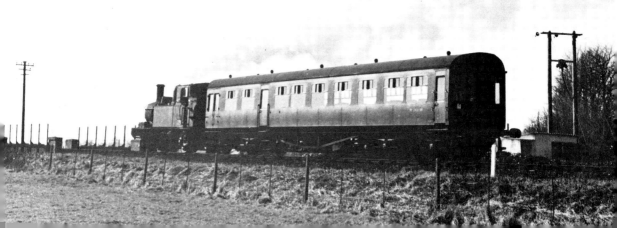

Left: A Sidmouth branch train bound for Exmouth seen between Sidmouth and Tipton St Johns in June 1949./*S C Nash*

Below: The 16.43 dmu to Exmouth at Tipton St Johns in August 1964./*Ian G Holt*

Right: Ivatt Class 2 2-6-2T No 41223 leaves Sidmouth with a daily goods train on a cold winters day in January 1965./*M R C Price*

Below right: The 12.15 dmu arrives at Sidmouth with a train from Sidmouth Junction whilst standard tanks Nos 80038 and 82035 wait to leave with empty stock from the 8.03 SO through train from Waterloo in August 1964./*Ian G Holt*

Above: The 11.50 Exmouth-Sidmouth train at East Budleigh with a through coach from Waterloo in June 1949./*S C Nash*

Left: Standard tank No 82022 approaches Woodbury Road *(renamed Exton Halt)* with the 16.20 Exmouth-Exeter Central train in June 1958. /*S C Nash*

Below left: The 15.35 dmu at Exton Halt with the Exeter St Davids-Exmouth train in January 1970. /*John A M Vaughan*

Right: Standard 2-6-4 tank No 80038 restarts the Exeter Central-Exmouth train away from Polsloe Bridge Halt in January 1963./*W L Underhay*

Exeter~Plymouth

Below: Class 3MT No 82013 assists Class 700
No 30691 from Exeter St Davids up to Exeter Central
with a mixed goods train in July 1960./*Frank Church*

Above: Class M7 No 30667 and 'Battle of Britain' class No 34060 *25 Squadron* leave St Davids with a stone train from Meldon Quarry assisted at the rear by two Class E1/Rs Nos 32697 and 32135 in August 1954./*H N James*

Below: Class U1 No 31903 restarts the 15.48 away from Exeter St Davids for Okehampton in August 1961./*Ian G Holt*

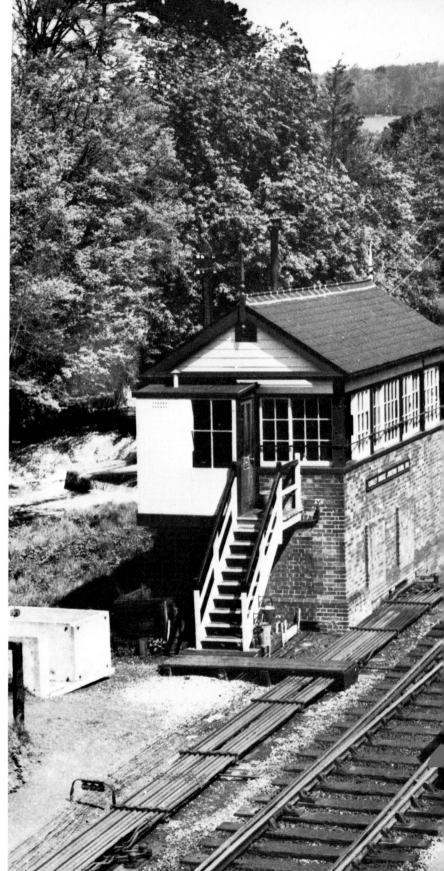

Between St Davids and Cowley Bridge Junction (Exeter) Southern trains traversed Western metals where it was possible to see westbound trains from Waterloo pass westbound trains from Paddington in opposite directions. Here 'Warship' Class 42 No 862 *Jupiter* passes Cowley Bridge Junction with a Plymouth-Waterloo train in 1964.
/M J Fox

Below: Again at Cowley Bridge Junction (note the new lay-out with single track) 'Warship' Class 42 No 813 *Diadem* joins the Western Region main-line with a freight train from Meldon Quarry in the early 70s./*J H Cooper-Smith*

Right: A train for Okehampton provides the Coleford Junction signalman with his water supply in January 1970./*John A M Vaughan*

Below right: Two T9s Nos 30712 and 30726 head an Ian Allan 'Trains Illustrated' excursion near Okehampton./*D S Fish*

Above: Class T9
No 30712 stands at
Okehampton locomotive
depot in October
1953./*R E Vincent*

Left: 'Battle of Britain'
Class No 34058 *Sir
Frederick Pile* draws into
Okehampton with a train
for Plymouth whilst a
connection for Padstow
waits at Platform No 1 on
the right./*P H Wells*

The impressive structure of tubular pylons and lattice deck girders forms the impressive Meldon Viaduct west of Okehampton. (*Right*) A Class U 2-6-0 crosses with a ballast train from Meldon Quarry in 1964. (*Below*) A 'West Country' Class 4-6-2 heads the Cornish portion of the 'Atlantic Coast Express' in 1962.
/*A J Wheeler, John Parsons*

Above: Rebuilt 'West Country' Class No 34026 *Yes Tor* approaches Meldon Quarry with the 8.41 Exeter Central-Plymouth train in June 1960./*S C Nash*

Below: Diverted off the Western Region the 10.00 Penzance-Paddington train passes Meldon Junction with 'Warship' Class 42 No 867 *Zenith* in charge in August 1961./*S C Nash*

The two-coach Plymouth portion of the 'Atlantic Coast Express' leaves Tavistock behind 'West Country' Class No 34017 *Ilfracombe* in October 1953./*R E Vincent*

Above: 'Battle of Britain'
Class No 34070 *Manston*
approaches Tavistock with
the 11.50 Plymouth-
Exeter train in April 1964.
/J C Beckett

Left: Class 2MT 2-6-2T
leaves Bere Alston with an
evening train for Plymouth
in April 1962.
/Brian Haresnape

Above right: 'West
Country' Class No 34036
Westward-Ho heads a
train for Plymouth
between Bere Alston and
Bere Ferrers in April
1954./B A Butt

Right: Class 4300
No 6318 arrives at Bere
Ferrers with a stopping
train for Plymouth in April
1954./B A Butt

Above: Rebuilt 'West Country' Class No 34097 *Holsworthy* makes its final approach into Plymouth along the banks of the river Tamar passing under the new road bridge at Saltash in April 1962./*Brian Haresnape*

Below: 'Battle of Britain' class No 34110 *66 Squadron* works empty stock out of Plymouth North Road in April 1962./*Brian Haresnape*

The North
Devon Lines

Below: 'Battle of Britain' Class No 34074 *46 Squadron* climbs the 1 in 37 incline from Exeter St Davids to Central Station with the 8.10 from Ilfracombe and Torrington which will then form the first part of the 10.30 up Waterloo train from Exeter Central in September 1958./*Colin P Walker*

Above right: 'Battle of Britain' Class No 34072 *207 Squadron* descends from Exeter Central with the Ilfracombe and Torrington portions of the down 'Atlantic Coast Express' in June 1959./*M Mensing*

Right: 'West Country' Class No 34029 *Lundy* waits for a clear road with an up meat train at Cowley Bridge Junction in July 1958./*R C Riley*

Below: 'Battle of Britain' Class No 34052 *Lord Dowding* approaches Crediton with the 8.35 Waterloo-Ilfracombe train in September 1954./*Peter F Bowles*

Although treated as a main-line provision had been made for double track along the single-line section between Copplestone and Umberleigh. The need for this never arose. Here 'West Country' Class No 34002 *Salisbury* nears Eggesford with the down 'Atlantic Coast Express'./*J C Beckett*

Above: Class T9
No 30710 shunts a pick-
up goods train at South
Molton Road in May
1952./*P H Wells*

Left: 'Battle of Britain'
Class No 34066 *Spitfire*
trundles a goods train
through Barnstaple
Junction.
/*Bryan H Jackson*

Above right: The
Ilfracombe portion of the
'Exeter Flier' special train
arrives back at Barnstaple
Junction behind Class
4MT No 80043 in October
1965./*Ron Fisher*

Right: 'Warship' Class 42
No 812 *Royal Naval
Reserve 1859-1959*
crosses the river Taw at
Barnstaple with the 8.48
Exeter St Davids-
Ilfracombe train in August
1968./*M Edwards*

Left: 'Battle of Britain' Class No 34060 *25 Squadron* climbs the 1 in 36 incline to Mortehoe with a train to Waterloo in the early 60s./*R Russell*

Right: Class 4300 No 6363 descends from Mortehoe with the 8.30 Taunton-Ilfracombe train via Barnstaple Victoria Road in August 1964./*S C Nash*

Below: 'Battle of Britain' Class No 34066 *Spitfire* heads the 16.50 Ilfracombe-Exeter Central train through the Slade Valley between Ilfracombe and Mortehoe./*J C Beckett*

Above left: 'Battle of Britain' Class No 34080 *74 Squadron* attacks the 1 in 36 incline out of Ilfracombe with the 16.50 train to Exeter Central in September 1963.
/J Scrace

Left: Class N No 31835 reverses back for a return train to Exeter after being turned at Ilfracombe shed in May 1959./*K L Cook*

Above: 'West Country' Class No 34024 *Tamar Valley* looks to be in need of a clean on the turntable at Ilfracombe shed in August 1951.
/J G Hubback

Right: 'Warship' Class 42 No 814 *Dragon* prepares to depart for Exeter in August 1968.
/David Burch

Left: Class 22 No 6338 enters Barnstaple Junction with a daily clay train from Meeth whilst a dmu waits to form the 12.38 to Exeter in July 1969./*J H Aston*

Below left: A Diesel rail-car enters Fremington with the 13.07 Barnstaple-Torrington train in September 1964./*Andrew Muckley*

Right: Class 2MT No 41283 leaves Instow for Torrington in July 1963./*R Cowlishaw*

Below: Class 2 MT No 41313 seen between Instow and Bideford with the 18.38 Torrington train./*J C Beckett*

Top left: Class M7 0-4-4T No 30256 heads the 9.25 freight from Barnstaple near Torrington in August 1955./*R E Vincent*

Left: Class 2 MT No 41213 waits at Torrington with the 12.10 freight train for Halwill in August 1963./*P Paye*

Above: A three car dmu forms the 'Exmoor Belle' special at Torrington in October 1970./*G R Hounsell*

The North Devon and Cornwall Joint Railway from Torrington to Halwill was the last addition to the Southern's West Country network. Opened in 1925 primarily to serve the numerous china-clay workings between Torrington and Okehampton. (*Right*) Crossing the river Torridge a double-headed train enters Torrington from Halwill in March 1965./*M York*

Left: Class 2 MT
No 41295 arrives at
Dunsbear with a train for
Torrington in June
1959./*J H Aston*

Below left: Class 2MT
No 41297 takes water at
Hatherleigh with a train for
Halwill in April
1960./*R N Joanes*

Right: The 'Exmoor Belle'
a special train sponsored
by the LCGB, RCTS and
the Plymouth Railway
Circle at Yarde Halt in
October
1970./*G R Hounsell*

Below: Class 2MT
No 41295 waits at Hole
with the 16.00 train to
Halwill in June
1959./*J H Aston*

Into Cornwall

Below: Class N No 31840 pulls away from Meldon
Junction with the 16.24 Okehampton-Bude train in June
1964./*J C Beckett*

Above: Class T9 No 30715 nears Dunsland Cross with a train from Bude to Okehampton in April 1960./*M J Esau*

Below: A dmu forms a train for Bude at Whitstone & Bridgerule in June 1966./*Ian Allan Library*

Above: Class 4MT
No 80067 stands at
Whitstone & Bridgerule
with the 13.55 Bude to
Okehampton train whilst
on the opposite platform a
Class N No 31837 leaves
with a train for Bude in
August 1963./*P Paye*

Left: Class N No 31836
stands outside the
locomotive shed at Bude
in August 1963./*P Paye*

Above right: Class T9
No 30715 heads the
15.45 Okehampton-
Padstow (SO) away from
Meldon Junction in
August 1959./*J C Beckett*

Right: The driver attends
to his engine No 30709
Class T9 at Egloskerry
with a train for Padstow in
April 1960./*R N Joanes*

Above: A Great Western Society 'North Cornwall Lines Farewell tour,' stops at Launceston in October 1966./*F W Crudass*

Left: The 14.25 diesel-rail car pauses at Otterham with a train from Halwill to Wadebridge in July 1966./*J Spencer Gilks*

Above left: Class T9
No 30715 waits at
Camelford with the Exeter–
Padstow train in
September 1959./
Derek Cross

Left: Class 1366 Pannier
Tank No 1369 shunts
wagons at Wadebridge in
August 1962.
/W G Sumner

Above: Class T9
No 30715 waits to leave
Wadebridge with the
16.25 school children's
train to Padstow whilst
class 4500 No 5572 runs
round its train from
Bodmin Road in
September 1959.
/P Treloar

Right: A Padstow train
leaves Wadebridge with
Class T9 No 30717 in
charge. Another T9 is
being serviced at the
Wadebridge mpd in
August 1959.
/Geoffrey F Bannister

Above: Class N No 31838 approaches Wadebridge with the 15.13 Padstow-Okehampton train in July 1963./*A W Smith*

Above right: Class U1 No 31904 waits to leave Padstow with the 15.13 to Okehampton in July 1961./*J Scrace*

Right: 'Battle of Britain' Class No 34070 *Manston* waits to leave tender first with the 14.52 Padstow-Bodmin North in July 1963./*A W Smith*

Above left: Class T9 No 30338 leaves Padstow for Wadebridge in April 1960./*Ian Allan Library*

Left: Approaching Wadebridge Class T9 heads the 14.20 Bodmin-Padstow train in August 1957. /*C Mogg*

Above: An empty railbus passes Nanstallon Halt heading for Wadebridge from Bodmin North in September 1964./*Andrew Muckley*

Left: Class N No 31842 leaves Boscarne Junction with a freight train bound for Bodmin General in September 1964./*J C Beckett*

The Wenford Bridge mineral line, England's second oldest railway, runs from Dunmere Junction to Wenford Bridge — the furthest outpost of the Southern 266 miles from Waterloo. (*Top right*) Three Beattie Well Tanks monopolised the working of this line. Here No 30585 makes its way through the woods near Penhargard with the 10.00 freight to Wenford in September 1953. (*Right*) No 3085 negotiates the crossing of the A389 with a train for Wenford Bridge in August 1959. (*Below*) A 'Train Spotters Joyride Special' made up of brake vans makes its way to Wenford not far from Dunmere Junction in July 1958./*S C Nash, G F Bannister, George W F Ellis*

Left: The 15.15 Bere Alston-Callington train crosses Calstock Viaduct into Cornwall in June 1961./*J C Beckett*

Above: Class 2 MT No 41206 waits to depart with the 13.00 train to Callington in August 1964./*Michael P Jacobs*

Right: Shunting at Callington prior to No 41206 going on shed for the weekend in August 1964./*Michael P Jacobs*

103

'The Cornubian' salute to steam special, makes the first recorded visit of a Southern 'West Country' Pacific on this section of the Western Region main-line at Bodmin by WC No 34002 *Salisbury* in May 1964.
/*D H Ballantyne*

The Odd One Out?
The Lynton and Barnstaple Railway

Below: Getting a double-headed train ready, two of the four Manning Wardle 2-6-2Ts *Taw* and *Yeo* at Pilton in 1935./*A B MacLeod*

Above: Taken from a series of early postcards depicting the L&BR in independent days. A view of Barnstaple Town Station with an early morning train for Lynton awaiting the arrival of a Southern train in the next platform./*R Antell*

Below: The operating headquarters with its offices, workshops, loco and carriage sheds, goods sidings and turntable were all contained at Pilton (Barnstaple). This view shows *Lyn*, the only American engine, outside the locoshed in 1935./*A B MacLeod*

Left: Yeo crosses Chelfham Viaduct in to Chelfham with a train from Barnstaple in 1935./*A B Macleod*

Below: Yeo seen this time at Bratton Fleming with a train for Barnstaple in 1935./*A B MacLeod*

Right: A view of Blackmore Gate looking towards Lynton./*R Antell*

Below: Parracombe water proved very good for locomotive purposes. Here *Lew* takes on water in 1935./*A B Macleod*

Lynton station, nineteen miles from Barnstaple, was
perched high on a hill overlooking the twin towns of
Lynton and Lynmouth. (*Above left*) Lynton, looking from
the Barnstaple end of the station. (*Left*) An early view of
Lynton showing the Swiss-chalet style station building.
(*Above*) *Lew* is ready to return with a train to Barnstaple
in 1935./*A B MacLeod, R Antell, A B MacLeod*

The Lynton and Barnstaple Railway was the first of the
Southern's services in the West Country to fall victim of
the motor car and was cut in 1935 and replaced by a bus
service. (*Above*) The last train to Lynton headed by *Yeo*
and *Lew* takes on water for the penultimate time at
Parracombe on Sunday 29 September 1935./*R L Knight*

Railways have rendered more services and have received
less gratitude than any other institution in the
land. *John Bright*